A TRIP TO THE FARM

HORSE FARMS

URSULA PANG

PowerKiDS press.

New York

Published in 2023 by The Rosen Publishing Group, Inc.
29 East 21st Street, New York, NY 10010

First Edition

Editor: Greg Roza
Designer: Leslie Taylor

Photo Credits: Cover kaband/Shutterstock.com; series artwork (background) OHishiapply/Shutterstock.com; p. 5 Sergey Novikov/Shutterstock.com; p. 7 Kalinina Alisa/Shutterstock.com; p. 9 ILiyan/Shutterstock.com; p. 11 Ivan Zelenin/Shutterstock.com; p. 13 Sjogger/Shutterstock.com; p. 15 LanaG/Shutterstock.com; p. 17 Alexander Oganezov/Shutterstock.com; p. 19 CatwalkPhotos/Shutterstock.com; p. 21 (clydesdale) Coatesy/Shutterstock.com; p. 21 (pony) Alexia Khruscheva/Shutterstock.com.

Cataloging-in-Publication Data

Names: Pang, Ursula.
Title: Horse farms / Ursula Pang.
Description: New York : Powerkids Press, 2023. | Series: A trip to the farm | Includes glossary and index.
Identifiers: ISBN 9781725339415 (pbk.) | ISBN 9781725339439 (library bound) | ISBN 9781725339422 (6 pack) | ISBN 9781725339446 (ebook)
Subjects: LCSH: Horses–Juvenile literature. | Horse farms–Juvenile literature.
Classification: LCC SF302.P364 2023 | DDC 636.1–dc23

Manufactured in the United States of America

Some of the images in this book illustrate individuals who are models. The depictions do not imply actual situations or events.

CPSIA Compliance Information: Batch #CSPK23. For Further Information contact Rosen Publishing, New York, New York at 1-800-237-9932.

CONTENTS

Hello, Horses! 4
Happy Horses 6
In the Stable 8
Horse Babies! 10
Hoof Care 12
Let's Ride! 14
Police Horses 16
Showtime! 18
Big and Small 20
Glossary 22
For Further Information 23
Index 24

Hello, Horses!

Have you ever visited a horse farm? That is a place where horses are raised and trained. They could be trained to do a job. Some are trained to carry riders. Some are trained to perform in **competitions**! Some horses are pets.

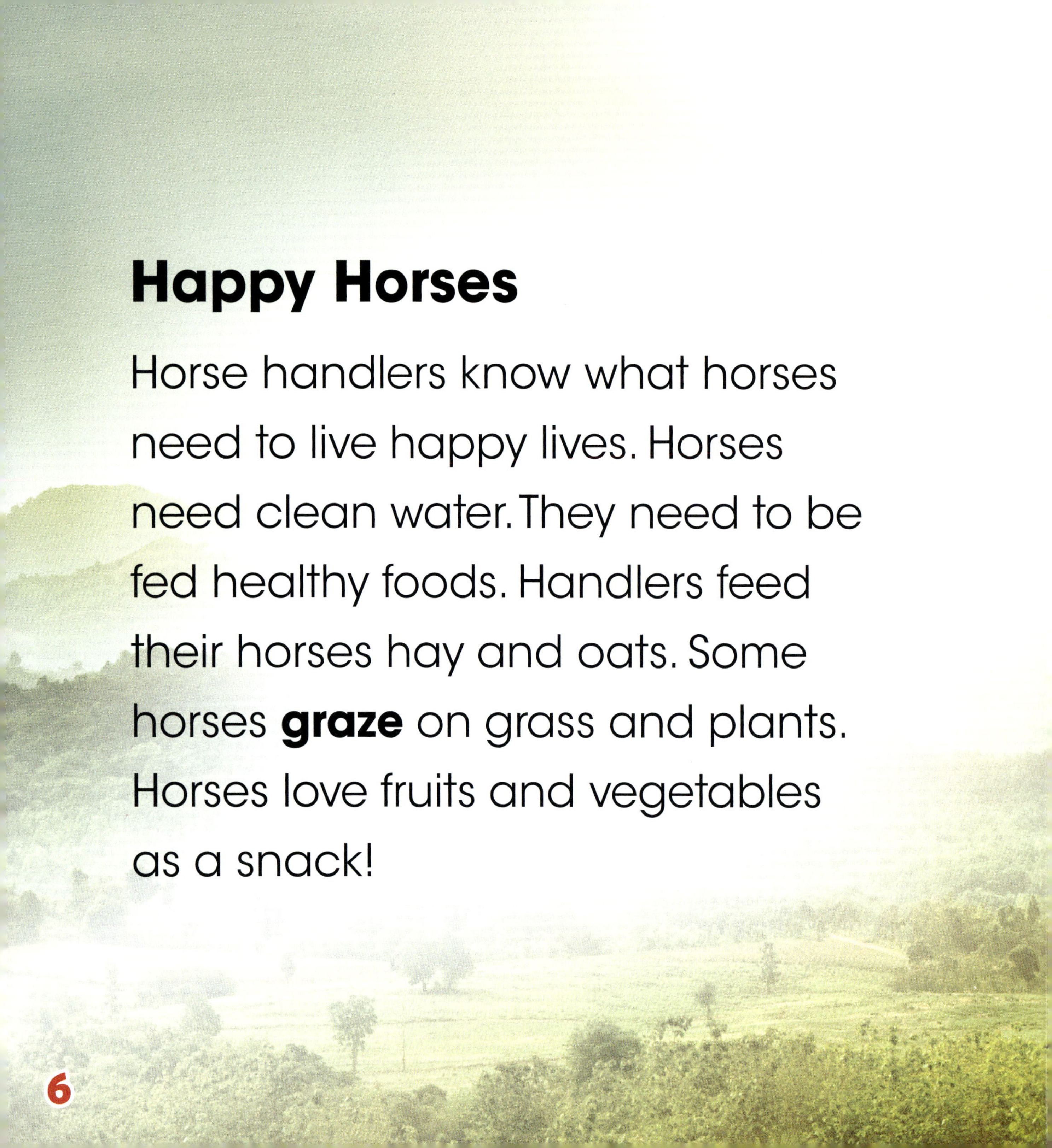

Happy Horses

Horse handlers know what horses need to live happy lives. Horses need clean water. They need to be fed healthy foods. Handlers feed their horses hay and oats. Some horses **graze** on grass and plants. Horses love fruits and vegetables as a snack!

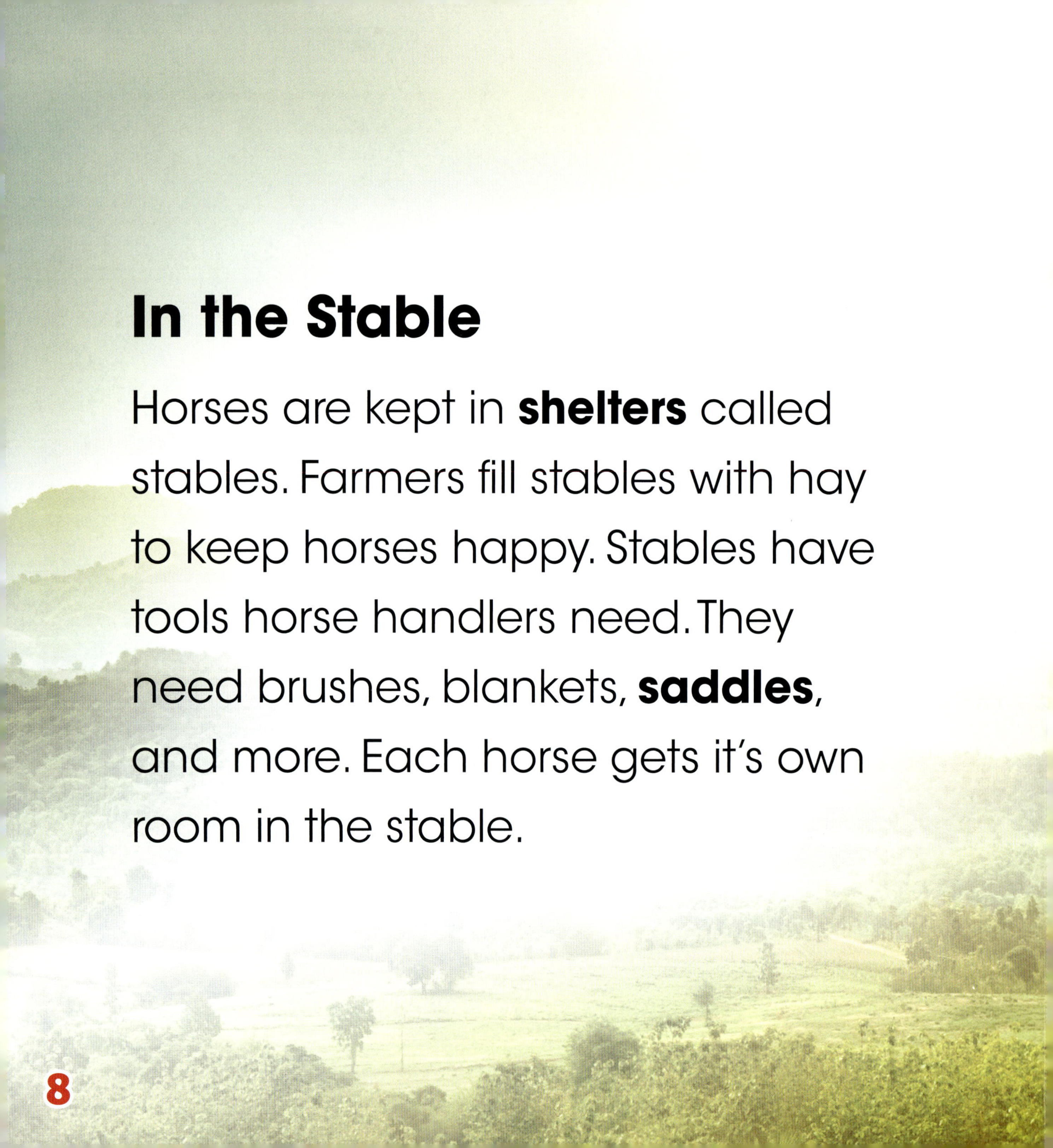

In the Stable

Horses are kept in **shelters** called stables. Farmers fill stables with hay to keep horses happy. Stables have tools horse handlers need. They need brushes, blankets, **saddles**, and more. Each horse gets it's own room in the stable.

Horse Babies!

The horses that live on farms sometimes have babies. A baby horse is called a foal. Farmers care for the mother and the foal to make sure they are well. Foals love to run and jump!

Hoof Care

Adult horses and foals need help caring for their hooves. Each hoof is like a big, thick fingernail. Horse handlers trim each hoof several times a year. Then they put a horseshoe on each hoof. Hoof care helps avoid **injuries**.

Let's Ride!

Many horses are trained to carry riders over trails for fun. Trail horses need to be friendly. They are good at listening to their riders. Trail horses aren't easily scared. They are good horses for people who are new to horse riding.

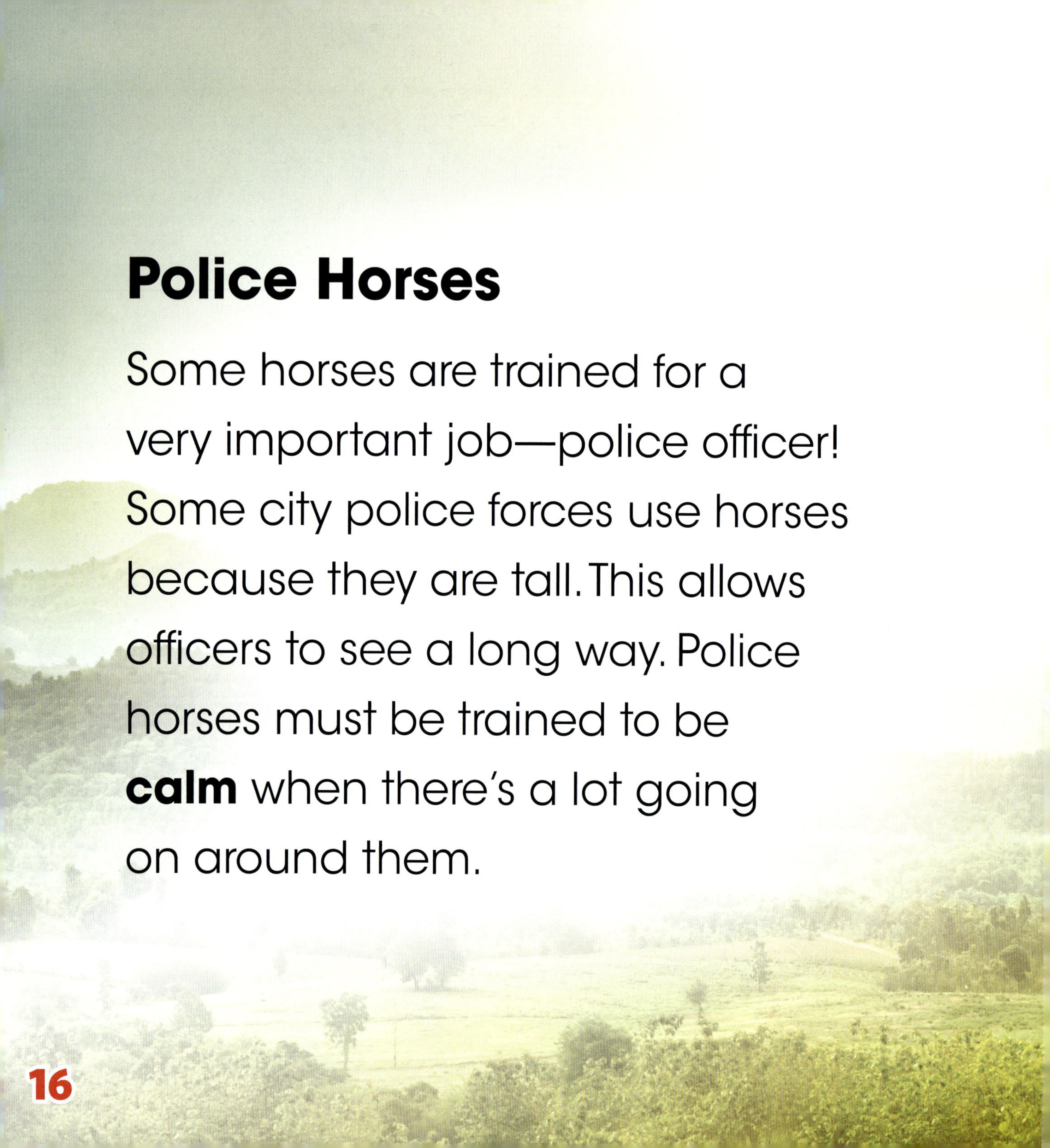

Police Horses

Some horses are trained for a very important job—police officer! Some city police forces use horses because they are tall. This allows officers to see a long way. Police horses must be trained to be **calm** when there's a lot going on around them.

Showtime!

Some horses are trained for competitions. They may race other horses. Some horses are trained to jump over fences. Dressage is a type of horse competition where the horses are trained to do difficult dances. Horses and riders must train for many years to get good at dressage.

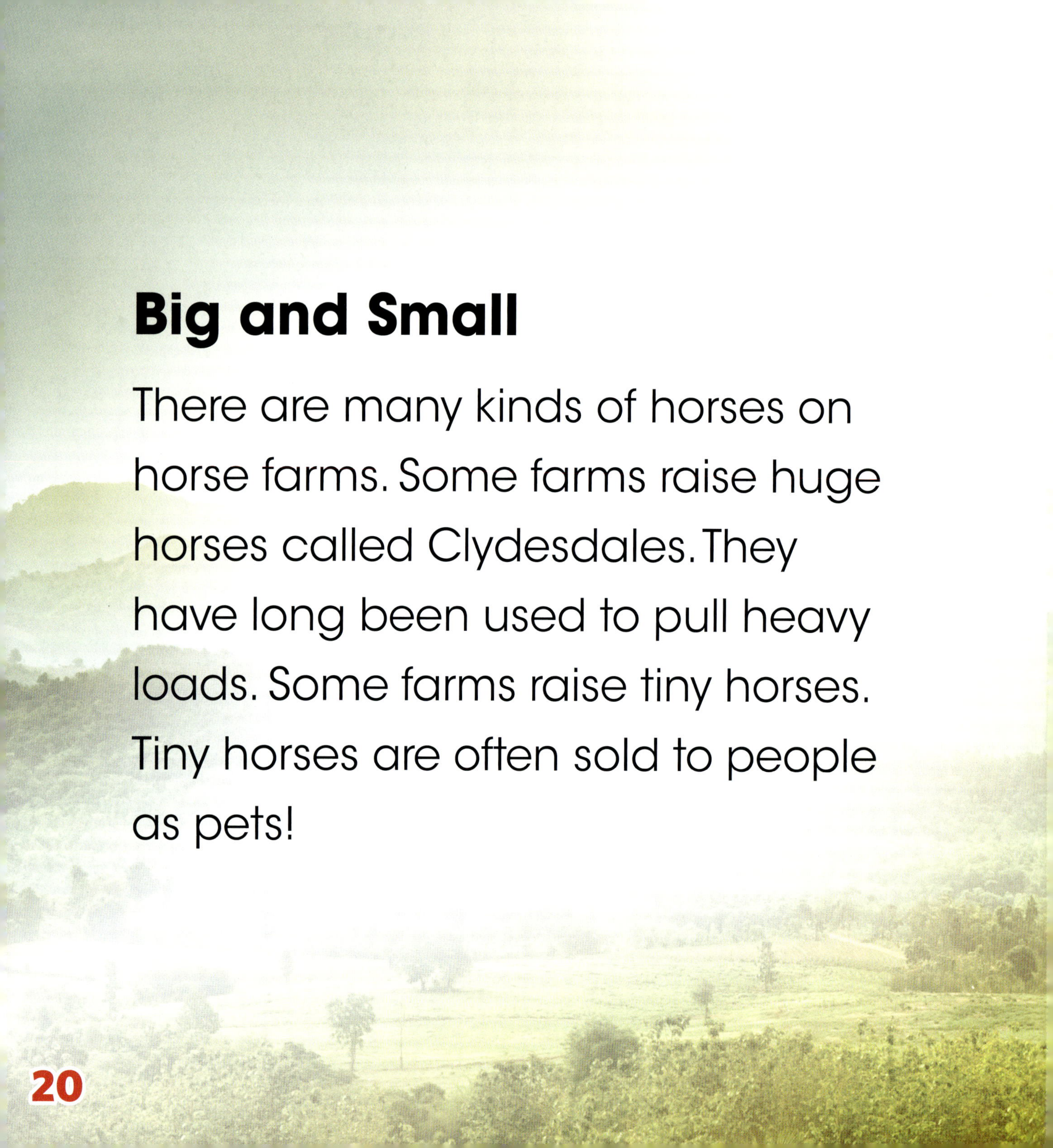

Big and Small

There are many kinds of horses on horse farms. Some farms raise huge horses called Clydesdales. They have long been used to pull heavy loads. Some farms raise tiny horses. Tiny horses are often sold to people as pets!

GLOSSARY

calm: Not excited or upset.

competition: The act or process of trying to get or win something others are also trying to get or win.

graze: To eat grass or plants growing in a field.

injury: Hurt or broken.

saddle: A seat made of leather that someone uses to ride a horse.

shelter: A building that covers people or things to keep them safe; a home.

FOR FURTHER INFORMATION

WEBSITES

Horses
kids.spcaeducation.org.nz/animal-care/horses/
Learn the proper way to care for horses at this detailed website. Includes fun facts about horses.

Horse Facts
www.konnecthq.com/horse-facts/
This website offers information about the different breeds of horses.

BOOKS

Jackson, Tom, and Diana Ferguson. *The Magnificent Book of Horses*. San Rafael, CA: Weldon Owen International, 2021.

Mortimer Children's Books. *The Book of Horses: The Ultimate Guide to Horses Around the World*. London, UK: Welbeck Publishing, 2021.

Publisher's note to parents and teachers: Our editors have reviewed the websites listed here to make sure they're suitable for students. However, websites may change frequently. Please note that students should always be supervised when they access the internet.

INDEX

C
Clydesdales, 20
competitions, 4, 18

D
dressage, 18

G
graze, 6

F
farmers, 8, 10
foals, 10, 12
food, 6

H
handlers, 6, 8, 12
hay, 6, 8
hoof care, 12
horseshoe, 12

I
injuries, 12

P
pets, 4, 20
police horses, 16

R
riders, 4, 14, 18

S
saddles, 8
stables, 8

T
trail horses, 14
train, 4, 14, 16, 18